D1794744

The Gift of Friendship

JOHN OSBORNE

The Gift of Friendship

A play for television

FABER AND FABER
3 Queen Square
London

First published in 1972
by Faber and Faber Limited
3 Queen Square London WC1
Printed in Great Britain by
Latimer Trend & Co Ltd Plymouth
All rights reserved

ISBN 0 571 10157 7

All professional inquiries in regard to this play should be addressed to the author's agent, Margery Vosper Ltd, 53a Shaftesbury Avenue London, W.1.

CAST

JOCELYN BROOME

EDWINA BROOME

BILL WAKELY

MADGE WAKELY

DANIELS

1 EXT.   DAY
English parkland half shrouded in late afternoon autumn
mist. A horse grazes in a paddock and lifts his head.

2 EXT.   DAY
The horse's head is turned towards the Georgian house,
which is the centre of the parkland.

3 EXT.   DAY
A window of the house. From behind a desk a man stares
ahead at the misty grounds.

4 INT.   DAY
The man, JOCELYN BROOME, *is seated at his desk in the*
library, opposite the window. He turns his attention from
the parkland to an envelope he is addressing. He writes
the name on the envelope in a careful, swift, neat hand:
'WILLIAM WAKELY ESQ., DOWN COTTAGE.'

5 INT. LIBRARY   DAY
A large clock strikes the hour of four. JOCELYN *finishes*
addressing his envelope, seals it with care and then
consults his pocket watch. He rises and goes to the door,
pauses, casting his eye over the shelves of books
surrounding his desk. He glances at one or two old
volumes and then his eye wanders to an extra row of two
or three dozen books, all with his name, 'Jocelyn Broome',
inscribed on the back. He takes one down, the first, and

examines it carefully. Then, from his waistcoat pocket, he
takes a key and a small card.

6 INT. LIBRARY C.U. KEY AND CARD DAY
On the card is written: 'May as well start at the
beginning. The end, as usual, is less interesting. Though,
perhaps, more instructive.' The key and the card are
placed on the frontispiece of the book, which is then
closed and replaced on its shelf with the others.

7 INT. LIBRARY DAY
JOCELYN *runs his fingers along the shelf. Then at an old*
school photograph of schoolboys posing as the football
eleven of that year. A group on a college green. The
young face of Broome with several others, all in army
uniform and posed beside an elephant and sepoys and
servants. BROOME *licks a stamp, which he fixes to the*
envelope to William Wakely Esq.

8 INT. LIBRARY DAY
JOCELYN *closes the door carefully and as he makes his*
way towards the hall and the front door, a voice from
the sitting-room calls out.

9 INT. HALL DAY
In the sitting-room JOCELYN's *wife,* EDWINA, *can be seen,*
looking up from her book. Although somewhat younger
than JOCELYN—*in her late forties—she looks the*
predictable wife for Jocelyn, with his waistcoat and
tweeds and red enclosed face.
EDWINA: You're early.
JOCELYN: No . . . same time.
EDWINA: Stint finished?
JOCELYN: That is not a question to ask a writer, especially after
nearly thirty years of married life. Besides, he's most
unlikely to tell you.
EDWINA: Some might.
JOCELYN: Indeed. But, I think you'll agree, I never have done so.

EDWINA: Going for your walk?

JOCELYN: I'm going to the post.

EDWINA: No walk today?

JOCELYN: No. Not today.

EDWINA: Very well then. I'll have tea ready when you come back. Are you sure you won't let Daniels post your letter?

JOCELYN: Quite. I'll not be long.

He pulls on an old tweed hat and coat, grabs a walking-stick, and, followed by a large, sleepy dog, goes out of the house.

10 EXT. GROUNDS   DAY

JOCELYN *strides a little uncertainly up the drive. He looks around him keenly, breathing the air very deliberately, patting the neck of the horse in the paddock, gazing back at the house and its still setting.*

11 EXT. POSTBOX IN WALL SURROUNDING THE HOUSE DAY

It is growing darker and a couple of cars flash by JOCELYN *as he hesitates by the box. He scowls at the cars, looks at the envelope with its name on it and then resolutely puts it in the box. He stares at the collection times as he hears the letter flop into the box. Then at the insignia 'V.R.' below. He makes his way slowly back to the gates of the drive, towards the house.*

12 INT. DINING-ROOM   NIGHT

JOCELYN *and* EDWINA *are dining alone.* DANIELS *is waiting at table.*

EDWINA: (*presently*) You're rather silent this evening, Jocelyn.

JOCELYN: What? Am I?

EDWINA: New book?

JOCELYN: No. Last one, more like. Or all of 'em.

EDWINA: Do you miss the children?

JOCELYN: *Miss* them. Good heavens, no. You must be getting old, my dear. It's taken me a quarter of a century to

get 'em all out of the house at the same time. Thank
you, Daniels . . . My father used to tell us he dreaded
the Long Vacation. Of course, we never believed him.
Thought we were an irresistibly amusing lot for him
to have around. That's why he kept sending us abroad
all the time. And if he couldn't persuade us to go, he'd
pack his old knapsack and go off on one of his walking
tours to Austria or some place.

EDWINA: Not so nice for your mother.

JOCELYN: Oh, don't know. Gave 'em both a rest, I dare say.
They did have sixty-one years of each other.

EDWINA: Well, yes—twice as much as us, I suppose. People
were closer then.

JOCELYN: Nonsense. They kept a respectful, sensible distance.
Not like our generation, always on about 'being in love'
and having affairs. As for this lot . . . like a lot of those
sea animals, huddled all over each other on the beach.
What do you call 'em, galapagos . . . lizards or something. Crawling all over one another. Crawling with
inertia and crowd . . .

EDWINA: Are you sure you're all right?

JOCELYN: I keep telling you so. I don't know what else I can do
to persuade you.

EDWINA: Only I could just catch the late train on Sunday and
get back here if you could meet me at the station.

JOCELYN: You know how I hate motoring, particularly at night.
No, you stay the night with your mother. I'll be all
right and Daniels will be here.

EDWINA: There'll be no one else. And the last time I spent the
night away, you were very poorly.

JOCELYN: Nonsense. Besides, I may not be alone. I may be
having a guest for dinner.

EDWINA: Really? You didn't tell me. Who?

JOCELYN: Wakely. I asked him to come and dine with me.

EDWINA: Bill Wakely? You mean—the writer?

JOCELYN: Naturally.

EDWINA: What about his wife?

JOCELYN: Which one?

12

EDWINA: Well, the latest, I suppose.

JOCELYN: Never met her. I only knew the second. She was pretty intolerable. Thought she was a better writer than him. Than either of us, for that matter. Ghastly woman, quite pretty in an intellectual housemaidish sort of way. Full of world problems and personal accusations. Even Wakely couldn't put up with her for long. Liked to give you the impression she was something of a modern scientific miracle in bed. Quite awful.

EDWINA: But aren't you going to invite the new one down with him?

JOCELYN: I don't see any reason to. Unlike him, I have a strictly limited curiosity. Which is why he'll come alone whether she likes it or not.

EDWINA: Women do change men's habits you know.

JOCELYN: Only weak or stupid men. I told him it was strictly on business.

EDWINA: But what business could you possibly have with Bill Wakely?

JOCELYN: Well, work then. After all we're both writers. In fact, I used to think him rather good.

EDWINA: But you haven't seen him for six years at least.

JOCELYN: That is no reason for not seeing him now.

EDWINA: But you used to be so close. Why now . . .

JOCELYN: I wish you wouldn't keep using that word. It has almost no meaning in the context in which you use it. One can be close to death, close to God, to one's wife occasionally, hardly ever with one's children, and, if one is really blessed with the gift, with a friend. Wakely has never been a friend, as you seem to make out.

EDWINA: Perhaps *he* thought so . . . I thought he represented all you despised.

JOCELYN: True. He began to. However, for a time we seemed to get some pleasure from each other's company. We went to the same college, used the same clubs, wrote for the same journals and magazines, shared the same profession and we're both apparently Christians. We didn't share the same regiment. As you know, while I

was serving, he edited a highly successful literary
magazine. He even published some of my stuff from
Burma.

EDWINA: He must have been younger than you. Why didn't
he——

JOCELYN: Join up? Some school injury so he told everyone.

EDWINA: You didn't believe him?

JOCELYN: Frankly, I didn't. But I never concerned myself with
it. Patriotism, like honour, is one's own business. I'll
probably hear in a day or so. If he accepts, Daniels
can make up a room. I dare say he'll stay the night.

EDWINA: Don't you want me to be here?

JOCELYN: Is there any reason why you should want to?

EDWINA: No. I never really knew him. I quite liked his work.

JOCELYN: He's skilful. And doesn't mind being entertaining.
Excuse me. I must go to the library, for a while. There
isn't a proof reader left to be trusted, it seems, except
myself.

EDWINA: Very well. I'll get on with my book.
She watches him go out.

13 INT. LIBRARY   NIGHT
JOCELYN *comes in, locking the door behind him. He takes
the first volume of his works down and extracts a key
from it. He then goes to a concealed safe/cupboard and
opens it. Inside are enormous piles of papers and note-
books. They are so meticulously arranged that they seem
almost untouched.* JOCELYN *takes down a heavy notebook,
rather like a ledger. On it is marked '1971'. He hesitates before closing the safe and takes down another
marked '1939'. He moves across to his desk, pouring
himself a glass of port as he settles into his desk chair and
lights a cigar. He looks up at a portrait of himself as a
young man in the style of, say, Sickert. Smoking his
cigar with obvious pleasure, he opens the volume marked
'1939'. He flips through page after page of the most, neat
careful handwriting.
Cut to various photographs of himself in 1939, in*

uniform and out.

JOCELYN: (*V.O.*) 14 November 1939. Tomorrow joining battalion. Heaven knows what else. Obviously, all kinds of things about to change or disappear altogether. Including oneself, although I must confess I don't feel it likely at this moment. Dined alone and very well. Unfortunate that Edwina didn't feel up to it, but no doubt due to the child's birth—and being somewhat difficult —as she said. Still, dining alone is still one of the most delicate and pleasing institutions of a civilized married life and I cannot pretend I was sorry, though naturally I was concerned about Edwina's health. But she is a strong girl, oddly, almost perversely mettlesome for one everyone says is so frail. She will outlast me, war or not. Not that I can complain. She is a good wife, especially for a writer, making the minimum demands and anticipating needs almost magically. Altogether, I must feel extremely favoured and, indeed, I actually feel it without any sense of self-delusion. I cannot believe the war will last overlong. My new book is what they call a best-seller. I have money in the bank; no obligations, save to my family, and, to my surprise and everyone else's, what appears to be a secure reputation as a 'stayer' as well as a stylist. All this and barely the age of thirty! The Good Lord has certainly done well by me. If he conducts the war as well as my career, it must surely end before Christmas.

15 November. Last night's euphoria gone. At least, for the day. Certain melancholy but inevitable, I suppose. (*He looks at wedding photographs of Edwina and himself.*) Edwina came to see me off, which I thought rather splendid. Not a tear but a lot of feeling at the same time. Beastly journey. Hear that Wakely is starting some news magazine. Rather the thing for him. I should say. Telling other people what they're supposed to be thinking. Believe he's all *for* the war now. Naturally, he won't join up until he has to. There are some who always believe in exemption. When, of

course, there is no such thing. As he will surely dis-
cover. His new wife sounds execrable.
(*C.U. photograph Wakely's wife.*)
Doubtless, she will not last much longer than the
previous one (whom I rather liked). Anyhow, it's unlikely that I shall have to meet her. Dined in the mess
for the first time. Wine quite passable, though food
beyond belief or comprehension.

14 INT. LIBRARY   DAY
JOCELYN *takes up his pen and writes an entry into the
1971 volume.*
JOCELYN: (*V.O.*) 19 October. Beautiful, misty day. The house
and everything around it looking at its very best. Term
time again and all those enormous children away. How
agreeable to be alone in such a place at such a time.
Except for Edwina, of course.

15 CLOSE UP   EDWINA READING FITFULLY

16 INT. LIBRARY   DAY
JOCELYN: (*V.O.*) But she is off to her Mama's soon, which will be
good for both of them. I pleaded work, which was
quite true as I think I'm getting back with things again.
Dined together and drank far too much of Cyril's
burgundy. Don't think Edwina noticed.

17 INT. PASSAGE   NIGHT
EDWINA *knocks at the library door.*
EDWINA: I think I'll go up now, Jocelyn. Try not to work too
late. Good night.
JOCELYN: Won't be long . . .
She goes up the staircase.

18 INT. LIBRARY   NIGHT
JOCELYN *stares at the door and pours himself another port.
He goes back to his journal, writing slowly.*
JOCELYN: (*V.O.*) Wrote to Wakely today, inviting him to dine on

16

Saturday. He can stay overnight as he'll surely not be
sober enough to drive back to London. Besides, his
curiosity will be too much for him after six years.
That's the journalist of the writer in him. I wonder if
he'll know how to deal with it to the best advantage.
We shall see. Naturally, I asked him down alone. Interesting to see what comes of it, if anything. I hear he
looks younger and better than ever. Perhaps it's all
these young wives. Rather than deal with all of that
I still prefer to be as I am, overblown, covetous and
full of smug forebodings . . .
(*He stares through his cigar smoke at the portrait of the
slim, romantic youth on the wall. Then goes over to
another shelf, taking down a book of photographs: pictures
of himself in long babies' robes; his mother and father;
playing cricket at his prep school. Holidays at Tenby,
1921, Zermatt, 1925 and so on. He takes the book back
over to the desk and opens it to show a group of three
young men in flannels on a college green. Underneath is
written 'Balliol 1932'. A young and identifiable Jocelyn
is on the left; beside him are two other young men. Each
one is identified: 'Broome; Wakely; F.L.E.' He stares at
the picture of Wakely.*)
Can't possibly look *that* much younger. Not after the
life *he's* led.
C. U. Wakely's photograph.

19 INT. RESTAURANT   NIGHT
BILL WAKELY, *almost forty years older than his Balliol
photograph but looking a trim, dissolute fifty rather than
a bland sixtyish, like Jocelyn. He is dining with his wife,*
MADGE, *who is even younger, and very attractive.*

MADGE: Well?
BILL: Well?
MADGE: Are you waiting to go?
BILL: No. Are you?
MADGE: You don't seem to be enjoying yourself much.
BILL: Well, I am—quite.

MADGE: Oh—quite . . .

BILL: Like most people who are supposed to have always pursued pleasure, I have always, really, when it comes to it, been prepared, no, more than prepared, to settle for very little. And, as for your*self*, anticipating in my little way that I do, the little turns out to be very considerable . . .

MADGE: Are you drunk?

BILL: Not drunk. I feel, oh, vaguely what I think usually is ill, but, as you know, I have never had what is called a 'serious illness' for forty years, let alone escaped being run over or shot at.

(*Pause.*)

I was twice covered in bits of wood and rubble and glass in cupboards under the stairs during the blitz; and I have never *quite* recovered from chronic dandruff and incipient acne.

MADGE: Oh, do shut up.

BILL: Sure . . .

MADGE: Sure . . .

BILL: I've told you before why writers are uninteresting.

MADGE: *Don't* tell me . . .

BILL: They are absorbed by yesterday *and* the day *before* yesterday.

MADGE: You're telling me . . .

BILL: And before that even . . . Future becomes more and more without meaning. Irrelevant to what you ever do . . .

MADGE: You certainly didn't enjoy the play tonight.

BILL: I didn't realize it was obligatory.

MADGE: What? Oh, not that.

BILL: You know . . . I've never cared much for plays.

MADGE: For people, you mean.

BILL: Actors aren't usually much like people. I've always thought.

MADGE: It's not your night at all, is it?

BILL: Never met many, mind you. What's that? No . . . But perhaps I might just prefer books to plays.

18

MADGE: Yes. I know: and literature to life. Come on. Let's go then.

BILL: Very well. But you're wrong.

MADGE: I've no doubt. Let's go.

BILL: Or perhaps *I'm* wrong. I'll have to get the bill first . . .
He waits and watches her, signs the bill, then they go out.

20 INT. BEDROOM   NIGHT
MADGE *and* BILL *prepare for bed.*

MADGE: So—*that's* it?

BILL: What's *it*?

MADGE: Jocelyn Broome was *it* all the evening.

BILL: No. He wasn't, actually.

MADGE: Why didn't you tell me before?

BILL: I was thinking about it.

MADGE: Is it that important?

BILL: Of course it isn't.

MADGE: What *is* important to you?

BILL: I've never really known.

MADGE: Is it me?

BILL: I dare say.

MADGE: You dare say . . .

BILL: I, well, it's like which is the worst of the . . .

MADGE: Not the best?

BILL: I was going to say—never mind.

MADGE: Yes?

BILL: Anything. Seven deadly sins. Worst of . . . Three graces—for the use of.

MADGE: Why do you want to go all that way for dinner, any-way? Seems a pretty insulting sort of invitation to me. As if he were asking you to go and mend his television set or something. No invitation to *me*.

BILL: He wouldn't.

MADGE: Well, why shouldn't he?

BILL: He's made a morality out of eccentricity.

MADGE: He's just a prig and a snob, that's what you mean.

BILL: And delighted he'd be——

MADGE: —to hear that I'd said it.

BILL: I never really knew him. I've told you.

MADGE: Is that why you talk about him so much?

BILL: He's a writer.

MADGE: So?

BILL: And a very fine one.

MADGE: There must be better or as good.

BILL: Not many.

MADGE: Not many that you knew once, were at Oxford together with and now, who probably despises you more than anyone and has never made any attempt to conceal it, at least, in the time I've known you.

BILL: That's not entirely—anyway——

MADGE: Anyway, *you* affect to despise *him* and always have done.

BILL: No. I haven't——

MADGE: At least, he's consistent. *He* doesn't spend years going around being hurt at being ignored. He probably delights in your criticisms. Look what you said about his last book.

BILL: I liked it.

MADGE: You didn't say so in your notice.

BILL: You wouldn't remember what I said.

MADGE: Who remembers what any of you says about one another? Or cares? You're only on about yourselves. Or them.

BILL: I told you. I liked it. And said so.

MADGE: Do you think so? Oh, I suppose you had it both ways, as usual, and managed to look clever and shrewd and non-oh-what-committal at the same time.

BILL: I don't know why you should make such a carry on about a dinner invitation.

MADGE: I don't know what it is, but it's more than that—at least, it is to you.
(*She reads from* JOCELYN's *note.*)
'Dear Wakely'—Wakely! Someone you've known for forty years nearly.

BILL: I shouldn't need to explain to you the intricacies of English social life, even if you were evacuated to

America during the war.

MADGE: Most amusing. While *you* were writing about Proust and Ezra Pound and Saint Beuve for the war effort.

BILL: Exactly—or almost—Jocelyn's point, I'd imagine. Or more. Certainly more.

MADGE: Yes, more. Well, go and find out more.

(*Reading again.*)

'I know that we have made no contact for some years, but it would oblige me if you could accept my invitation to dinner on Saturday. I don't think you have been here before—no, you haven't—so I am enclosing a map of the area, which I think makes it fairly clear how to get here by road. I don't imagine you will come by train, although I have always found it most pleasant. My wife, Edwina, whom you may remember, will be away for the week-end, so we shall dine alone. If you wish to stay overnight, it can be easily arranged. Please send a telegram if you are unable to come.' *If* you are unable to come. He knows you'll go.

BILL: No, he doesn't.

MADGE: He gambles, like you all do—when he knows the odds. Go then.

BILL: Thanks.

(*He turns out the light.*)

I may. No . . . I think I will.

21 EXT. MOTORWAY DAY

BILL *in his car.*

BILL: (*V.O.*) Thus it was, as they're supposed to say in Victorian novels—or is it only television adaptations? —anyway, that I er—I——

(*He glances round at the cars speeding past him on, it seems, all sides.*)

—found myself driving down—a little uncertainly— to Jocelyn's for dinner. I'd had a frosty lunch with Madge, who'd managed to invite herself for the weekend somewhere, presumably as a riposte to my accepting the dinner invitation. As a result, I'd had an extra

half of wine too much, to say nothing of the rest, and
I seemed to be trapped on all sides by honking machines
of tin biting their way over me, like flies passing from
horse to horse and field to field. I soon realized I
wasn't up to the fury of it all, and eventually des-
cended rather aimlessly but thankfully down a turn off
and on to a secondary road that I thought must lead
somewhere in the direction of Jocelyn's rather grand
but discreet Palladian house.

22 EXT. JOCELYN'S DRIVE   EVENING
BILL: (*V.O.*) If Palladian can be discreet. I, along with most
of my friends—friends?—well, people who knew
Jocelyn, pretended it was even more vulgar in his
particular tenure. But then most of us had week-end
places, all mod-con, we called 'cottages'. Anyway, it
looked impressive enough, no, quite inviting even, in
the early October mist. Some people would have you
believe—including myself sometimes—that England
was already no more than strip of concrete and
rumbling stench. I was passing houses where the
people had never been to Bristol or Cheltenham, let
alone London. Maybe there weren't many but there
were some still left. Sometimes it's as if we smash our
favourite gifts, simply for the pleasure of saying: look,
it's broken. Jocelyn wasn't that kind of 'smash all your
delicate plates and you'll feel better' school. He hid
away what he valued most. Hoping that erosion would
almost certainly be cheated by death. Or, at least for
himself and a few careful, tidy spirits of his own
generation. In the future, he had no interest whatso-
ever, and, as I drove up to the house, still a little
befuddled by lunchtime wine and week-end drivers, I
began to think I saw why and something like, oh,
almost, longing came over me. To see. To see him just
once again. I'd no regrets about alienating my wife or
inciting her to plunge off into some contact-greedy,
semi-humanity grasping clutch of idle week-enders,

desperate and probably hurt—hurt or inert. Inert in their hurt . . . God, I *was* feeling ropey. *And* late. Punctuality was one of Jocelyn's tiresome affectations. Though, I must say, he managed to carry it off without seeming too schoolmasterish. I just hoped he'd not go through the pretence of not remembering he'd asked me. I'd sent him a very carefully worded telegram. I wanted a reviving drink, a longish meal and talk with the old boy and then maybe a hot bath and bed. Even Jocelyn thought hot baths were one beneficial product of modern life.

23 INT. DINING-ROOM   EVENING
DANIELS *is taking away* JOCELYN*'s plate.*
DANIELS: Shall I wait a little, sir?
JOCELYN: Wait a little? For what?
DANIELS: Your guest, sir.
JOCELYN: What guest?
DANIELS: Mr. Wakely, sir.
JOCELYN: What are you talking about?
DANIELS: A car has just driven up, sir.
JOCELYN: Then go and see who it is.
He looks at his pocket watch as DANIELS *goes out to the hall and admits* BILL.

24 INT. HALL   EVENING
BILL: Good evening. I'm late but expected, I think.
DANIELS: Yes, sir. Mrs. Broome told me to expect you, sir. Your room is made up—in case—sir. Mr. Broome is in the dining-room. Perhaps you'd care to join him now, or——
BILL: I'll go straight in.

25 INT. DINING-ROOM   NIGHT
JOCELYN *is watching* BILL *through his main course as* DANIELS *hovers.*
JOCELYN: I always dine at 7.45. Otherwise I get no sleep at all.
BILL: Why shouldn't you? Bloody week-end drivers.

DANIELS: (*darting in*) Finished, sir?

BILL: What? Oh, yes. All right.

(*He clearly hasn't and grasps his claret glass to him for comfort. As the two men talk,* DANIELS *continues to serve the rest of the meal, discreet, but, all the same, a presence.*)

BILL: (*V.O.*) Wish that bloody Daniels character would disappear. What's old Jocelyn up to. Food's good, no, it's fine, but not all that good. Not *that* journey. And rowing with Madge. We could have had a lark of some sorts at *her* week-end place; even a quick tuck-up and titter as we used to say. Used to . . . What's he up to. Does he *like* being thought of as a—what, yes, oh clever buffoon, ex-stylist, reactionary—except they don't call it that nowadays. Wonder if I should give Madge a ring. Oh, I suppose he doesn't *have* one, like the telly and the radio.

JOCELYN: We've no television. I know you think that's an affectation.

BILL: No.

JOCELYN: Edwina occasionally listens to a play on the wireless, if it's not too late. She will probably call me soon. If you want to talk to your wife, by the way, Daniels will get you the number. We only have one instrument.

BILL: No, thanks. I seem to remember that when Lord Curzon was Foreign Secretary—or was it—Chancellor —he had only one instrument—in the butler's pantry. He had to walk about half a mile from his study to the staff quarters to talk to the P.M.

JOCELYN: How clever of you to remember.

BILL: My name is George Nathaniel Curzon,
I am a most superior person,
My flesh is——

JOCELYN: Cheek is——

BILL: Pink.
I dine at Blenheim twice——

JOCELYN: Once only——

BILL: A week.

24

JOCELYN: Masque of Balliol—1881.
  BILL: Well, we've all something to answer for.
JOCELYN: I think we'll take port in the library this evening,
         Daniels.
DANIELS: Very good, sir.
   BILL: (*V.O.*) Monday will be hell. Let alone tomorrow. I've
         not spoken to him yet, let alone her.
         (*To* JOCELYN.)
         I think I *will* just give Madge a ring. Just let her know
         I've—see if she's all right.
JOCELYN: By all means. Daniels . . .

        26 INT. SMALL, CHEERLESS ROOM   NIGHT
           BILL *on phone. To* MADGE.
   BILL: Madge? Sorry I didn't ring before but I was late
         getting here and then Jocelyn insisted on getting his
         damned dinner on time. And, there's only one tele-
         phone, of course . . .

        27 INT. GUEST BEDROOM   NIGHT
           MADGE *is on phone.*
  MADGE: I'm surprised you got there at all in your state.
         Having fun, are you?
   BILL: (*V.O.*) What?
  MADGE: Fun.
   BILL: (*V.O.*) I don't think it would be your idea of fun or
         mine either.
  MADGE: Sorry.
   BILL: (*V.O.*) Anyway, we've scarcely spoken yet.
         (*She looks down at her feet in silence. Pause.*)
   BILL: (*V.O.*) You still there? Madge! Madge . . .
  MADGE: Yes.
   BILL: (*V.O.*) Are you all right?
  MADGE: Fine.
   BILL: (*V.O.*) Having a good time?
  MADGE: Not specially. I think I'll go back downstairs for a bit
         then go to bed.
   BILL: (*V.O.*) You could have done that at home.

MADGE: I could have. But I didn't . . .

BILL: (*V.O.*) Shall I try and get back tonight and you make an excuse or something.

MADGE: What's that?

28 INT. ROOM NIGHT

BILL: It's bloody cold in this place.

MADGE: (*V.O.*) That's what comes of aping the upper classes. There'll probably be *steam* on the bathroom mirror. (*Pause.*)
Perhaps you'd better get back to Mr. Broome before he gets into his nightgown and cap.

BILL: Perhaps you're right.

MADGE: (*V.O.*) What?

BILL: She can hear better than that! Better than I can. Lousy bitch.

MADGE: (*V.O.*) Are you talking to Jocelyn or to me? It's difficult to make out.

BILL: Oh, don't bother. I'll see you sometime.

MADGE: When? What's your number?

BILL: It doesn't matter. No one can hear it or will answer it. Pleasant dreams. And try not to damage the hostess's furniture.
He puts the phone down.

29 INT. GUEST BEDROOM NIGHT

MADGE *puts the phone down. Next to the bed, on the table, is a book clearly marked 'Private—First Edition'. She turns to the title-page. In it is a clear inscription from Jocelyn to Bill. ' "New occasions teach new duties"? Perhaps. But "Time makes ancient good uncouth"? We shall see. Your affectionate, as ever, admiring friend. J.B. August 1938.'*
She takes out a cigarette, lights it and then burns the pages of the fairly frail book, dropping the remains, still burning, into a waste basket, where it burns placidly enough. Then she crosses the room, opens the door to the sound of music and voices below.

26

INT. JOCELYN'S LIBRARY   NIGHT
He stands by the fireplace, below his own youthful por-trait, talking to Bill.

JOCELYN: Do have some more. (*Pours port.*) Did you get through all right?

BILL: Yes. Thank you.

JOCELYN: Nothing wrong? Telephone always means something wrong to me. All right for business men, I suppose, being important, ringing up Europe or New York and California at all hours. Placing orders or confirming contracts or whatever they do. Nothing to do with people like us. No . . .

BILL: No.

JOCELYN: I hate this time of day, don't you. Actually, before dinner slightly worse. At least, after dinner, you can get off to bed. If you can sleep, which I can't. I take some pills from the quack. Don't approve of 'em—or me taking 'em, that is—but they don't seem to *do* much anyway. Can't read much in bed. Can you? Not many decent books. Keep reading the same ones. Do you read much new stuff? Yes, I suppose you do. I never wrote about other writers much. Mostly, when you used to ask me, as a matter of fact, and I've always tried hard to stop 'em writing about me . . . but they go on . . . writing your obituary before you're dead, and then there's little else to add to what's been said. Have you ever read an *interesting* obituary—I mean one you'd read again? No. . . . No, you see I get so devilishly bored with Jocelyn Broome. With Broomie. By the late afternoon, it's almost too much. I go for a walk every day but you can't escape it. Can you? (*He stares out at the parkland.*)

BILL: No.

JOCELYN: There you are.

BILL: There we are . . .

JOCELYN: Not you. You've a young wife, you keep on with your work, you go on, travelling, lecturing . . .

BILL: Like some sort of cultural travelling salesman?

JOCELYN: I hadn't thought of it that way. But you—I see your
point . . . No, I can't sleep. Perhaps it's too much to
ask. Like a lot of other things. Nothing to be done
about it. No choice or chat—like what they call 'going
decimal'. . . . Being decimated. . . .

BILL: Broome. We haven't dined together for ten years
nearly.

JOCELYN: Really? I'd no idea it was so long, my dear fellow. It's
the curse or blessing of getting older.

BILL: Yes, I know. Ten years can seem like a day. . . .

JOCELYN: Ah—yes. Banalities. I tried to avoid them in my work.
By exercising style. Craft. So much laziness and so
laborious. So much fat and effort and overlength gone
into it all. My son—the one at Balliol.

BILL: Vivian.

JOCELYN: Yes. What haughty little names we used to choose for
ourselves: Vivian. I think that was Edwina's idea.
And Jocelyn. What? Oh, yes. Vivian sent me this book
about a certain J.C.—'just an ordinary cat doing his
own thing, who gets caught up with another cat, Judas,
an'—what is it—(*he reads*)—it's on the jacket—'an
idealistic pop plugger worried about his boy. With
Pilate, an amiable square who keeps washing his hands
to a really fantastic group. Get yourself a cross, baby,
and just stretch out and turn on. . . . That's after a
mind-busting number called Gethsemane: "God, you
giving me such a time. These old words don't ever
rhyme." ' Then there's—oh yes—'Mary Magdalene,
like she says just "screw". Isn't that great? Followed
by visions, sex, you name it. And finally, Brother, tonight we shall all have our thing in Paradise. So screw
your vinegar and hyssop. Remember, Che rose again,
too.' . . . I know it's another banality, but we *did* have
the finest language in the world. Once. We didn't set
such a good example, I dare say.

BILL: *You* have.

JOCELYN: The actual labour of *writing* books is more or less
finished. Even reading proofs and printing. No one has

28

'time'. Time . . .

BILL: You didn't ask me here to talk about 'time'.

JOCELYN: You're a writer. You know the drudgery and the tire-someness of it. There aren't many of us left, so there's not much importance to it all. Or is there? I think we're giving away a lot, don't you. Laziness. We *all* suffer. I tried to be diligent. So did you. Death still has terror, don't you think. Even for those like you—or, indeed myself—the ones who drift into it. Drift. Drift. Drifting . . . How different from idleness. Watching a bird descend across my window. Or staring at the portrait. Not with much pleasure. But a pretty long, wasting appraisal. Why did we sit at these sort of desks, looking at that sort of English countryside we've embraced around us, just for the sake of a few thousand words unmemorable to everyone but a few friends and professors in over-endowed American universities. We are both right. Why dinner? Yes: I want you to be my literary executor. What an absurdity it is. Rather like being the guard on an obsolete railway train. More?

BILL: Please. I think so.

JOCELYN: Have you noticed that politicians never refer to death? Obvious I suppose. . . .

BILL: One must, what, accept the brutal limitations of one's medium? The tyranny of one's mistakes. Oh, that sounds like one of those reviewers' weekly aphorisms you despise so much.

JOCELYN: Yes. It does. But it's, yes, right, for once. It is difficult, difficult to accept. After a lifetime of careful, minute attention to one's work, one's way of life, the centre of every day's attention. Copying, correcting, striking out. Yes, striking out, risk-taking. Literature is a little like mining. Ever thought of it? Obvious—but what is not . . . That's true. Boom! Everyone buys, rushes, invests, all in a frenzy of some kind of enlightenment. Then the seam runs out. The inspiration trickles, the novelty, the insight goes, the earth fails. Itself. It fails like a

water supply, a tap—dripping into silence. It simply
. . . goes. Goes. Pearls that were once, say, a great
price, become commonplace and a drug on the markets
of time. I read somewhere of people—like us—being
something like the light of the world. . . . How nice it
is of you to come. I get extraordinarily tired. I've
written one or two goodish books, though.

BILL: You've done that.

JOCELYN: Yes. Perhaps. I don't *think* you're being polite. We're
never that to each other. Politeness is *not* the gesture
of friendship. . . . And, somehow, I can't help feeling
that, at a strict distance, in a landscape, that is, we
have had feelings of friendship for one another. If not
accord.
(*Pause.*)
Do I seem as dotty to you as everyone says?

BILL: No.

JOCELYN: You're wondering why I asked you down. No whim, I
can assure you of that. I really must go to bed soon.
You *were* somewhat late. But I *mustn't* chide. What
was it? Oh, I've got this clean first edition. I want to
give it to you. I gave you one once before—at least, so
I remember.

BILL: I still have it.

JOCELYN: Do you? Really? I'm glad to hear it. Thought you
might have sold it. No. I didn't. My price will go up.
Then down, very quickly.
(*He gives* BILL *a copy of one of his own books. Inside is
written:* 'To W.W.: not so much one of the seven as the
eight. Although the seventh led to it—clearly. J.B.')

BILL: Thank you.

JOCELYN: Forgive me, dear fellow. I've brought you all this way.

BILL: It's been good to see you.

JOCELYN: No. It can't have been. I shall have probably gone for
a walk when you get up. Or to church. Do remember
me to your wife. We've not met, have we? No. Nor
shall I expect. Now. You've got the book?

BILL: Yes.

30

JOCELYN: Why does one feel so on edge at this time?

BILL: On edge with Broome, you mean?

JOCELYN: Yes. Exactly. Oh, I—I want you to be my literary executor. It's a lot to ask, isn't it?

BILL: Rather.

JOCELYN: Awful drudgery and digging about in places you may not like or care for.

BILL: Why, well, why me?

JOCELYN: You? Default, I dare say. Do you mind?

BILL: No. But it may not arise.

JOCELYN: Oh, it will.

BILL: You're not—planning anything?

JOCELYN: What? Oh, no—events will take their own course. So: you'll do it?

BILL: Yes.

JOCELYN: Good. Thank you. I'm sorry if I put it in such a churlish way. But, you see, I really trust no one. Which is a sad admission. Like withdrawal of faith. Or grace. Not even you. I have had an enjoyable and highly successful marriage but this is not something to saddle Edwina with. There are areas of our lives we have carefully preserved from one another. And, I think, rightly. In most cases, and particularly in the most private, the most secret aspects of my work. Marriage would be impossible without such secrets. Anyway, I don't wish her to be burdened with them.

BILL: Only myself?

JOCELYN: Yes. Do forgive me. One gets into these drab habits in the country. An odd fatigue can settle on one.

BILL: I'm quite aware of it.

JOCELYN: I'm sure. Daniels will get you anything you want. Good night—Wakely.

BILL: Good night—Jocelyn.

JOCELYN *looks hesitant, then seems to go out as quickly as he can. Almost guiltily.* BILL *looks down at his book.*

31 INT. STAIRCASE NIGHT

BILL *goes up to his room. He knocks quietly on the door.*

Then, hearing nothing, goes in, and recognizes his
pyjamas, etc., and closes the door behind him. He tosses
the pyjamas aside and closes his eyes, lying on top of the
bed. A lighted cigarette in his hand.

32 INT. BEDROOM NIGHT
BILL wakes up, stubbing out his cigarette on the table
beside him. To his horror, he finds he has burnt it out on
the fly-leaf of JOCELYN's *book.*
BILL: Oh—no!

33 INT. BEDROOM MORNING
BILL, still dressed, puts the book into his suitcase. He
looks out of the window and sees the rather doddery figure
of JOCELYN, *with hat, overcoat and walking-stick. In the*
early mist. A lone bird flies downwards.
BILL: WELGAPS . . .

34 INT. DINING-ROOM DAY
BILL *and* MADGE. BILL *is reading* The Times *obituary*
column: 'Mr. Jocelyn Broome.'
BILL: (*reading*) 'As a novelist, and more as a literary per-
sonality, he often gave the illusion of being more a
figure of the nineteenth century, whereas he was, in
fact, an innovating ironist of unique style, without ever
descending into modishness in his work. Although he
seemed to have adopted an almost eccentric, purple
melancholy, it never seriously affected the familiar
style of his particular, fastidious wit. He leaves a widow
and five children. . . .'
MADGE: You didn't like him.
BILL: No. Not much.
MADGE: He didn't like you either.
BILL: No. But he *was* friendly—the last time.
MADGE: Dotty, you mean.
BILL: Yes. Pretty dotty. But he did some pretty good things.
MADGE: Yes. But you didn't say much at the time.
BILL: No. I didn't. I thought I did. But, looking back on it

—I looked at the cuttings—no, you're right. I didn't.

MADGE: He went his own funny little way. No, not little. He went after himself. Instead of others. That's what you all do. Harry the others. Hector them. Right to the grave. You used to call him arrogant. But you know he wasn't.

BILL: No. You're right. Arrogant he wasn't.

MADGE: What was WELGAPS?

BILL: What? Oh, the way I remembered the seven deadly sins. Wrath, Envy, Lust, Gluttony, Avarice, Pride, Sloth. I think it was Sloth that bothered him. And another one.

MADGE: Are you going to the funeral?

BILL: I think not.

MADGE: Good. I don't think his spirit would somehow welcome you.

BILL: No.

35 INT. COUNTRY CHURCH   DAY
EDWINA *watches coffin proceed down aisle. She glimpses* BILL *at door alone.*

36 INT. BROOME'S HOUSE   DAY
EDWINA *shows* BILL *into the library.*

EDWINA: Well, I'll leave you to it. I suppose you'll know what you're looking for. . . .

BILL: I hope so. Thank you.
(*She goes out. He goes to the shelves and takes down several volumes of* BROOME'*s work. On the fly-leaf of each is written the initials 'J.B.' after, in order: 'Wrath';* '*Envy'; 'Gluttony'; 'Avarice'; 'Pride'; then 'Sloth'.* BILL *takes down another volume. On it is written: 'Ambition. J.B. Which led to the seventh.' Inside is the key to the cupboard-safe.*)

37 INT. BILL'S STUDY   NIGHT
BILL *is studying a file of papers, marked 'Broome— Jocelyn' on the various files.* MADGE *comes in.*

33

MADGE: Well? Not coming to bed?

BILL: Not for a bit. Do you want to hear any of this?

MADGE: Is it interesting?

BILL: As interesting as—a lifetime. Someone's struggle.

MADGE: To work? Instead of something about someone else. (*She sits opposite him.*)

BILL: (*reading*) 'Stress. Writing no longer a pleasure. Doctors no use. Quacks, diet or exercise. Memory. Not good. When does it start to go. Can remember distant past. But not yesterday. Edwina hardly. Will write to Wakely. Getting so clumsy. Hate clumsiness in others. Why should I tolerate it in myself? No, I shan't. Will write to Wakely. Why does he spend his life writing about *others*? Writing about others. Being a literary commercial traveller.'

MADGE: Ah.

BILL: 'I wonder if he despises me as much as I feel I should him. What a frightful sentence. Must stop talking to myself. . . . But there's no one else. Really. Can't talk to Edwina.'

MADGE: Not surprised.

BILL: 'Let alone Wakely. Will get rid of him quickly. He's bound to be late.'

MADGE: Right again.

BILL: 'And I can pretend to be more daft than I am. Oh, good Lord, I wish you *were* the light of the world. It's becoming all very dark indeed. Mustn't talk to myself. Too much food. And, of course, alcoholic Wakely looks very good, I hear.'

MADGE: Not that good . . .

BILL: 'Better to give up than be patient. . . . I never listen much anyway. Better to give up than even try to be patient. . . . Nervous habits. Must get to bed early. Otherwise, I twitch. Yes—just twitch. Edwina's used to it, but someone like Wakely, would make too much of it.'

MADGE: He *did* know you.

BILL: 'Must get away from noise. Noise. Listen, even the

door closing is no comfort any longer. Shouldn't hate trivia. But I do. Whatever is TRIVIA. Myself, most of all? Surely. Go to bed. Tired. Wake up just the same. Pretending I've done something. Done nothing. Just fatigue. No proper effort. Can't sleep but tired. No quacks. No pills. Won't work. No pleasure in writing. Not much from reading. At least lust gone. Only SLOTH. Ambition gone quite certainly. Wakely will, at least, save me from those American professors. At least, I hope so. Those LADEN universities and their LADEN students. EXEGESIS. Lord, I give myself to the Wakely, but not the WAKELYS of this world.'

MADGE: He's welcome.

BILL: Now this is the bit. 'There are only two finalities. Is that what I mean? Hell and America. The United States and Despair. What a shabby little creature Wakely is. Fawning on everyone because he is so scared—no, in anguish, at the idea of being left out or ignored. Sucking up to people he thinks are going to "make it". Sometimes, I give him a crumb of praise or, even more effective, aloofness, self-parody and downright contempt. He laps it up. Like they all do. As if any of it matters. Or could.' Madge . . . He really hated me. For thirty years. Nearly. And I never knew. Thirty years.

MADGE: Yes? Perhaps there's a lot people like you fail to notice.

BILL: I thought, at times, that I might have been of help. Or—even peripheral encouragement.

MADGE: It's a point of view.

BILL: Yes.

MADGE: After all—that's how you make your living.

BILL: How?

MADGE: Having a point of view. And putting it down for the world. You should think about it. Maybe it's his legacy to you.

BILL: But he really, *really* hated me.

35

MADGE: Are you surprised?

BILL: Yes. Oh, yes. I am. You think he was—not right? But —what?

MADGE: He felt it. And you made him feel it. So: it was true to that extent. What about those American universities?

BILL: No. This lot is for *me*. Besides, he made his wishes pretty clear.

MADGE: Good. If you can do that when *you* die, you've done pretty well. See you later. . . .

She goes out. BILL *stares at the pile of papers and picks out the volume marked 'To W.W. from J.B.: Sloth.' From paper: 'Time does not make ancient good uncouth.'*

FADE OUT